# What America's Teachers Wish Parents Knew

# What America's Teachers Wish Parents Knew

Compiled by
## Judy and Tony Privett

LONGSTREET PRESS
Atlanta, Georgia

Published by
LONGSTREET PRESS, INC.
A subsidiary of Cox Newspapers,
A division of Cox Enterprises, Inc.
2140 Newmarket Parkway
Suite 118
Marietta, GA  30067

Printed in the United States of America

1st printing 1993

ISBN 1-56352-104-0

This book was printed by Data Reproductions Corporation, Rochester Hills, Michigan.

Cover design by Amy Wheless
Book design and typesetting by Laura McDonald

This book is dedicated, with love, to
my two super children—Matt and Meredith—and to
my wonderful dad, Earl D. Eblen.

J. P.

I dedicate this book to the many teachers
who made a difference in my life, and especially to George
and Mary Grace Privett, great parents, friends,
and teachers.

T. P.

## ACKNOWLEDGMENTS

We wish to send our sincere thanks and gratitude
to the following educators who made this book possible:

Natine Abreu, Catherine Adams, Lynda Ade, Laurie Albro, Diana Allen,
Della Anderson, Janet Anderson, Nancy Anderson, Stan Angle,
Beverly Arnold, Art Aronsen, Thomas Asbury, John Ashton,
Richard Atwill, Barbara Baker, Lana Baker, Judy Ball, Babs Barham,
Laura Barnett, Judy Ferris Barro, Robert Barzdukas, Marilyn Baxter,
Melva Beasley, Shirley Beberniss, Kathryn Bell, Kimberly Bell,
Carolyn Belson, Linda Bengtson, Norma Bernstock, Rose Besser,
Judy Bielizna, Susan Billen, Paul Billiard, M. Jane Black, Rachel Blake,
David Boomgaard, Tom Bosman, Alice Boudreaux, Ann Marie Bradford,
Katherine Bradshaw, Jennifer Bragg, Lois Branche, Laurel Brinks,
Rhonda Brixius, Ruth Brown, Alice Browning, Rosemarie Burns,
Rose Ann Buschur, Thomasann Butler, Kelly Byrd, Shirley Byrd,
Judy Byrne, Tonya Caldwell, Karen Campbell, Patti Carter,
Timothy Cartwright, Judith Cassetta, Deb Cates, Robin Chesnut,
Gail Clemons, LouAnn Clifford, Brenda Coffelt, Betsy Van Sidden Cohen,
Shelcia Collier, M. Colvin, Stanley Comer, Jan Conine, Roy Connor,
Michelle Cook, Karenina Cooper, Sheila Cooper, Charlotte Corcoran,
Amy Gore Cox, Nancy Coyle, Marcia Cummins, Deborah Cunningham,

Diane Dalton, Betty Damer, Judy Dampier, S. J. Daugherty, Irene Davis,
Mary Jane Davis, Tanya Davis, Loretta Walker Davis, Mary DeBower,
Mary Lynn Decker, Rick Denmon, Debra Dennisuk, George DiMundo,
Pam Dinkins, Beth Dodd, Rosalee Dolan, Cheryl Zimmerly Donohue,
Linda Doody, Barbara Dorff, Aida Dorr, Mary Driskill, Thomas Dubrish,
Cyd Duffin, Barbara Duncan, Karen Dvorak, Kim Easter,
Anastasia Eldredge, Lee Epps, Connie Erholtz, Rosa Escamilla,
Marguerite Ann Evanko, Ava Ezell, Mary Kay Farr, Mary Faulkner,
Wilfred Faulkner, Frances Faulks, Sherley Fisher, Rosalind Flicker,
Gayleen Flood, Linda Francis, Cynthia Freeman, Joe Freeman, Cindy Frick,
Lynn Gallagher-Main, Joan Gansebom, Paula Garcia, Dana Garnett,
Ann Garrett, Maria del Rosario Garza, Cathy Gaudio, Barb Gilhaus,
Peggy Gillard, Liz Gottlieb, Dana Gravley, Debbie Green, Nancy Green,
Sandi Groppenbacher, Judie Gustafson, Christine Guy-Lambert,
Carol Hadorn, Kaye Hagler, Beverly Hague, Gina Hahnel, Betty Hamblin,
Patricia Hammell, Kimberly Handley, Karen Harrell, Cheraye Harris,
Jane Hartling, Debra Hartvigsen, Lillian Hawkins, Barbara Hazard,
Carol Heffley, Bill Allen Heim, Judy Heimer, Emily Helms, Audrey Henry,
Corene Herbster, Alicia Hingston, Susan Hinton, Kelley Hirt, Stacy Hirt,
Timothy Hite, Mary Holder, Connie Holliman, Sherry Ann Hopkins,
Ruth Ann Horn, Mike Hovenic, Courtney Tews Hoversen,
Consi Swan Hudson, Tom Hudson, Janice Hughes, Karen Hull,

Virgie Hunter, Cindy Hutchins, Patricia Leffler Hutchinson, Jean Ingle,
Mary Janice Jenkins, Brenda Johnson, Clarence Johnson, Karen Johnson,
Mariel Johnson, Joyce Jones, Glenda Kampwerth, Lisa Kaplan,
Jan Karcher, Elaine Karl, Holly Karte, Ann Kehner, Beckee Keller,
Ruth Kelly, Judy Kern, Katharyn Klein, Rhonda Knerr, Lee Knuckles, Sr.,
Kris Komatz, Paul Koops, Alice Krasow, Diane Kroack, Judy Kuhel,
Heidi Larsen, A. Lauro, Nancy Law, Jennifer Lawson, Edna Leath,
Patrice LeBlanc, Lynne Lecrone, Ronald Leese, Jean Leid, Kerri Levi,
Alta Ruth Lockman, Joy Logan, Bonnie Lovell, Connie Lowe, Wanda Lowry,
Pauline Lundeen, Helen Lyness, Tom Mack, Robert Malchow, Shari Maline,
Louise Malinowski, Ellenjo Noonan Malloy, Dee Ann Margrave,
Carol Marine, Kay Marsden, Goldie Martinez, Lisa Massey, Helen Matta,
Clifford May, Brenda Mayer, Esteen McAlister, Susan McBride,
Deah McCoy, Carol McCray, Patricia McDonald, Nancy McGowan,
Judith Anne McGrath, Maria McHorney, Johnnie McLaughlin,
Sharon McLaughlin, Maria McNamara, Kathy Meador, Mimi Medvetz,
Janice Walzer Meehl, Ruth Meier, Bridget Mellinger, Deborah Michieka,
Von Middleton, Jim Mielke, Cheryl Miller, Jean Miller, Susan Miller,
Mildred Jackson Mills, Laura Mitchell, Dorothy Mongo,
Michaeline Morella, Dee Morgan, Horace Morgan, Maria Morgan,
Karen Moulder, Donna Bell Mullen, Bette Murdock, Maura Murphy,
Bettyann Murray, Jeannette Murray, Rita Murry, Tina Neal, Carol Nelson,

Mary Jo Newell, Jim Nicholson, Helene Nickel, Maxine Nix, Susan Nix, Catherine Nodoro, Bill Norton, Cornelia Bryant O'Neal, Carl Oberholtzer, Patricia Oglesby, Keith Olszewski, Andrew Osborne, Tara Singletary Osborne, Katherine Denham Osgood, Linda Ott, Jacqueline Riley Owens, Rochelle Packard, Rebeccah Paget-Decker, Cindy Palmer, O. Pando, Lorraine Papa, Annette Parker, Darlene Parker, Debra Parr, Myrna Parsons, Karol Patterson, Wanda Pessini, Beverly Peterson, Janice Peterson, Annette Pettit, Myrna Lea Pickard, David Pilegg, Mary Jo Pingley, Mary Pinkham, Sandra Pittaway, Sonna Pitts, Ann Pope, Julia Porter, Pamela Poteete, Debra Prince, Marion Pritchard, Sue Pritchett, Denise Putman, Dianne Quinn, Wendy Raineri, John Ranone, Peggie Ravida, Reba Reading, Tom Reedy, Glenda Reeves, Jill Reierson, Karen Rembold, Virginia Rhodes, Paulette Rogers, Miriam Rohrbaugh, Priscilla Romo, Myrna Rose, Susan Rosen, Sandra Ross, Patricia Rowe, Oliver Ruff, Barbara Sabin, Ginger Salomone, Joan Savoia, Cathy Sayer, Don Schedler, Linda Schneider, Lynn Schroader, Tim Scott, Sue Scrivner, Veronica Semko, Leslie Shear, Judy Shepard, Ron Shepherd, Gene Sherman, Beth Shipp, Mike Shklar, Susan Sigmon, Alice Silvey, Genevieve Simpkins, Dianne Sizer, Thomas Sledge, Sr., Sheryl Smith, Betty Sue Snyder, Dorothy Solberg, Amy Spangler, Fran Spencer, Susan Spurlock, Judy Staley, Carol Stanford, Robin Stateler,

Debbie Stewart, Kathy Stewart, Holly Stinnett, Elizabeth Stocks,
Esther Joy Stone, LaVaun Story, Shirley Stott, Darlene Stotts, Gail Stover,
Cindy Sullivan, Linda Sullivan, Karin Swift, Diane Szelazkiewicz,
Larry Tag, Corliss Talley, Jr., Daniela Taylor, Darlynn Terry,
Dorothy Terry, Barry Thomas, Sharon Thomas, Carolyn Kay Thompson,
Delores Thornton, Glojean Benson Todacheene, Otto Tufenkjian,
Karen Turner, Margie Tuthill, Barb Van Slyke, Jessie von Leer, Joy Walker,
Elvira Walters, Wanda Wandress, Barbara Ward, Betty Ward,
Brenda Ward, Isabel Wechsler, Rhea Weinbrom, Nancy Weiner,
Sue Weller, Russ Werth, Dave Wertz, Janet Wheatley, Pam White,
Joan Whitney, Areta Williams, Elaine Williams, Holly Wilson, Mike Wilson,
Pamela Faye Wimer, Marcia Wolf, Larry Wolf, Andy Wollman,
Ann Hunt Wood, Rebecca Ann Woolard, Patrice Wright, Chris Wyscaver,
John Young 3rd, Patricia Young, L. Zeitchick, Joan Zimmerman

And for helping us get out a huge mailing, a very special thanks to:

Amanda Alvarado
April Alvarado
Kim Creager
Nicole Meador
Meredith Tucker

# INTRODUCTION

After more than ten years as a CPA, my wife, Judy, decided to return to school to get her teaching certificate. Years of involvement in her children's schools as well as substitute teaching had convinced her that a career in education would offer more fulfilling rewards.

During the course of her studies one evening, we were discussing the various theories of education she was required to learn. Judy related them to the numerous theoretical books she'd read on "how to parent," and said, "What we need to do is ask teachers about our children—after all, they often spend more time with them than we do."

The book you hold in your hands is the result of that thought.

We asked teachers from more than 6,000 schools in all fifty states to tell us the one thing they wish parents knew. From practical tips on how to help your child read and write, to handling the complex emotional needs of adolescents, teachers wrote their "wishes" with passion.

While the national media is focusing on the symptoms of dropping test scores, we found teachers are still begging parents to treat the disease by reading to and with their children. Our responses show overwhelming recognition that *the parent is the first and most important teacher*, and they follow with dozens of practical suggestions for making the best use of that responsibility.

When do you praise, and when do you discipline your kids? How do you sort out the differences between your child's and the teacher's versions of events that happen at school? Humor, straight talk, and thought-provoking ideas make this a practical handbook for parents with children of any age.

Read on, parents . . . America's teachers have something to say.

# What America's Teachers Wish Parents Knew

# I WISH THAT PARENTS . . .

would realize the tragic irony in the fact that sixteen years of education was required of me before I was allowed to teach their children; yet their job as a parent, which requires no education at all, is so much more important than mine.

7TH GRADE LANGUAGE ARTS

could wake up one morning as their children and live through their child's day at school.

5TH GRADE

would allow their child to fail. I know that sounds odd, but too many parents make excuses for any error a child makes. As adults we make mistakes and think nothing of them. When children do something wrong, some parents find a reason or think it wasn't their fault.

KINDERGARTEN–6TH GRADE P.E.

1

would not make promises they cannot keep. You've never seen a sadder face than a child's whose mom or dad promised to come have lunch with him and, for some reason, was unable to come. Try saying "I'll try, but I can't promise."

KINDERGARTEN

would realize that when children are having problems at school, they already feel bad about it and don't need to feel worse when they get home.

7TH–9TH GRADE ENGLISH

knew that if a child read for 60 minutes a day, he could increase his standardized test scores by 90 percent. Reading for 30–40 minutes a day would improve scores considerably.

3RD–5TH GRADES

# I WISH THAT PARENTS...

knew what kids say at school about them. Parents should believe only half of what's said to them about school. Always check it out with the adult source—the teacher—for clarification.

2ND GRADE

would not send a note with their child saying, "If Johnny gets sick, have him call me to come get him." Guess what happens *every* time. That's right. Johnny gets sick and has to call home.

KINDERGARTEN

realized that their last contact with their child tremendously affects that child's self-concept and desire to learn on that day. Whether it is the night prior or the morning before they leave, make it positive and loving. Don't underestimate love!

1ST GRADE

would be careful not to get into the habit of always giving excuses for students not having work done. All too often a student's learning disability becomes the "reason" for everything the child does wrong. Children quickly learn from the models set for them.

4TH GRADE

knew how important the first five years are in a child's life. So much about a child (attitude toward learning, reading and language skills, psychological well-being, socials skills, and self-esteem) is already in place by the time she enters school. Kids are pretty accurate mirrors of the environment in which they've grown up.

2ND GRADE

# I WISH THAT PARENTS . . .

wouldn't criticize their children or compare their abilities because the children will only learn to condemn.

would ask their children daily what they did at school and then wouldn't accept "nuthin'" as an answer.

would *never* demonstrate their child's name in all capital letters. I wish parents would teach children from the first moment of holding a pencil to write their name with the first letter only as capital. Teachers spend months *re*teaching this in kindergarten and 1st grade.

# I WISH THAT PARENTS . . .

would agree not to undermine the other parent when a divorce takes place. A child's self-esteem depends on how he sees both parents. Let the child know he doesn't have to take sides.

KINDERGARTEN–4TH GRADE GUIDANCE COUNSELOR

would become more actively involved in their children's education by visiting schools, supporting homework and discipline policies, volunteering to help in any way possible, and helping us teach students "The 4 R's":

Rights, Respect, Responsibility, and Relating

MIDDLE SCHOOL PRINCIPAL

would believe only half of what their child tells them about the teacher! I only believe half of what their child tells me about them.

1ST GRADE

# I WISH THAT PARENTS . . .

would remember the anticipation of the first day of school, the excitement of a field trip to a zoo, the agony of failing a math quiz, and the satisfaction of coloring a picture without going outside the lines.

2ND GRADE

would *read* their children's homework before they sign it for approval. We get homework written diagonally across the page, splattered with tomato sauce, or with little brother's artwork included . . . and still get Mom or Dad's "seal of approval."

2ND GRADE

would beckon to their children from ahead, rather than pushing from behind. Use less physical and more mental energy.

4TH GRADE

# I WISH THAT PARENTS . . .

would listen to what teachers are saying. In the old days, if a student got in trouble in school, he or she would be in trouble at home. Nowadays if a student gets in trouble, the parents want to know what the teacher did wrong.

I am not saying the teacher is always right and never makes a mistake, but parents could at least reserve judgment until they have heard both sides of the story.

4TH GRADE

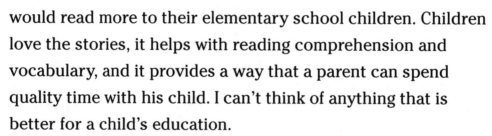

would read more to their elementary school children. Children love the stories, it helps with reading comprehension and vocabulary, and it provides a way that a parent can spend quality time with his child. I can't think of anything that is better for a child's education.

1ST–6TH GRADES

# I WISH THAT PARENTS . . .

knew how confusing the concept of odd and even is to children. When I asked if any of my third graders could tell me what they know about odd and even, one of them proudly said, "Odd was the man who ate the apple that his wife Even gave him."

1ST–3RD GRADES

· ——— 🎓 ——— ·

could hold onto their teenage attitude of how important it is to talk about everything and how important it is for someone to listen. Parents lose their children's respect when the focus on listening—without judgment—is lost.

7TH–12TH GRADE LIBRARIAN

· ——— 🎓 ——— ·

would remember how thin bedroom walls are. Children hear what is said behind closed doors.

9TH GRADE HEALTH EDUCATION

# I WISH THAT PARENTS . . .

would encourage scholarship in their sons and daughters with the same fervor with which they encourage gymnastics, dancing, and baseball skills. Wouldn't it be great if moms, dads, or nannies (since everyone seems to have one these days) had to rush their kids off to "Pop Warner" algebra, or "Little League" essay writing?

9TH–12TH GRADE MATH

·———— 🎓 ————·

would tell their children that "down south" is not a city and state.

6TH GRADE

·———— 🎓 ————·

understood the best thing to do behind a teacher's back is to pat it.

1ST–6TH GRADES

# I WISH THAT PARENTS . . .

would never tell their children, "I was never any good at math when I was in school." The mountain that I climb as a math teacher is much steeper when self-confidence begins to erode years before my work begins.

9TH–12TH GRADE MATH

would encourage honesty in their children by setting an example. I had a parent who swore that her child's missing homework had been completed at home and that she had personally checked it. The student and I later found the assignment (unfinished) in the bottom of his locker. The student confessed it had never gone home! The most important lessons are not the content of subject areas but those of values and character.

3RD–6TH GRADES

would help their child feel important and invincible. The child who thinks he can climb a mountain will most likely do it.

KINDERGARTEN

would learn to *let go*. Sad little faces crying at the classroom door, pitiful looks of abandonment, hanging around the halls, peeping through windows, prolonged kisses at the door, and repeated declarations of "I love you" have got to stop. Parents, your behavior is embarrassing. Get a grip!

KINDERGARTEN

knew that quality education begins before conception and belongs to that child who receives from his healthy, drug-free, emotionally stable parents an inheritance that continues through all stages and ages of development.

KINDERGARTEN

knew just how much teachers want to be a partner in their child's educational experience. Our school has implemented a home visitation program for teachers. In an effort to evaluate this program, we sent parents a letter asking for their reaction. Many favorable comments were received. One parent responded: "It was nice having you in my home. We got the most cleaning done this week that we have all year." I think this shows just how far some teachers will go to be in a partnership with parents!

7TH AND 8TH GRADE READING

appreciated that children spend only 18 percent of their yearly learning time in school. The remaining 82 percent of time, the parent is the teacher. Think about the difference you make!

KINDERGARTEN–3RD GRADE

# I WISH THAT PARENTS . . .

would make sure they knew what their kids were bringing with them to school. I once had a student who brought his grandfather's dentures to class, and being something of a class clown, put them in his mouth. Naturally, they got stuck.

2ND GRADE

would turn off the TV and provide more family-oriented activities such as: going to the library, reading to the children, playing board games, and cooking with them. Parents don't seem to spend quality time with their children anymore—some rarely talk to them . . . except to tell them to turn the TV down.

KINDERGARTEN

would increase their awareness of the sensitivity of children and teenagers. Harsh words can inflict mental damage.

10TH–12TH GRADE SCIENCE

# I WISH THAT PARENTS . . .

taught their children to love without fear, show compassion for others without reservation, and respect diversity in race, creed, and color.

3RD GRADE

·——— 🎓 ———·

would recognize the value of their children's art. Like the child, her artwork is unique, one-of-a-kind, irreplaceable, and priceless. Please encourage, value, and cherish their artistic creations.

KINDERGARTEN–5TH GRADE ART

·——— 🎓 ———·

could see life through their children's eyes. Life is not logical and task oriented, it's whimsical and multifaceted. Find out what your children are interested in (you may be very surprised) and let them explore.

12TH GRADE ENGLISH

15

would say *no* to the question "Can I stay up a little longer?" Tired tots are terrible to teach!

KINDERGARTEN–2ND GRADES

realized that TV is the Great Distorter. It either presents a fictional world that has little basis in reality, or it presents a world of hyper-realism in which every flaw in human relations is magnified. Children watch this, and some of them, anchorless as they are, have no hope of connecting with the real ground zero. The more they watch, the worse it gets.

6TH–8TH GRADE ART

would always remember to instill in their children the beauty of life, the miracle of love, and the wondrous magic of an education.

1ST GRADE

knew what a joy teaching can be when you're having an extra busy or tough day and one of your students says, "I love school," or signs a letter to you, "Your friend and good kid."

4TH GRADE

knew that second-grade male teachers like myself are not just "kindergarten cops," although we sometimes fit that description. We can be as loving and caring as any female teacher, in spite of how many times we are hit, bit, kicked, pinched, punched, or thrown up on. All of these have happened to me during my twelve years of teaching, but I love and care deeply about every student I have taught.

2ND GRADE

would not criticize their child's teacher in front of the child.

2ND GRADE

would be more realistic about grades. Just because your child needs an A or B to go to a specific college does not mean I will give it to her. The student must earn it. When she has done that, her pride, self-esteem, and feelings of self-worth will carry her further than any grade not earned.

11TH AND 12TH GRADE CHEMISTRY

would at least let the student do his homework in his own handwriting as they dictate the answers, instead of thinking I can't tell the difference. It is very obvious when the answers are in cursive and the class has not yet moved beyond manuscript.

3RD GRADE

would not force their children to participate in competitive athletics.

6TH–8TH GRADE SPECIAL EDUCATION

# I WISH THAT PARENTS . . .

would understand that after spending 180 hours or more with their children, we sometimes get attached to them and treat them as our own. That's why I sent your daughter to her room.

9TH–12TH GRADE SPECIAL SERVICES

would take the time to know and love their child as we teachers do. There are some great young people (contrary to what we so often hear)!

7TH–8TH GRADE LANGUAGE ARTS

knew that every comment they make about me is repeated at school. Since I am pregnant, I have heard many comments about my weight! Many of my students' parents would just die if they knew that I knew!

KINDERGARTEN

would send their child to school with an encouraging, positive "good-bye" each day. Examples:

> Be a good listener today.
> Be a good worker today.
> Try your best.
> Try to listen and follow directions.
> Learn something new to tell me about this afternoon.

Try to avoid:

> Get 100 percent today.
> Have fun!

The last remarks you make to your child each morning are reflected in her attitude and effort throughout the day. There are times when school is "fun" or exciting, but most of the time it requires a lot of work and effort on your child's part.

1ST GRADE

realized how devastating negative comments (put downs) are to the egos of early adolescents.

7TH–8TH GRADE COUNSELOR

would remember to encourage their children to try their best at whatever they attempt and to instill a desire to better themselves.

3RD GRADE

would teach their children to tell the truth, admit when they are wrong, accept punishment respectfully, be diligent and conscientious in all endeavors (whether they like it or not), and help dispel the attitude that teachers are the enemy.

9TH–10TH GRADE ENGLISH

would return to school (periodically and unannounced) to observe their child and the teacher. It's called "Shock Time"!

9TH–12TH GRADE SOCIAL STUDIES

would listen when their child comes to talk to them. Also, try to see the world through your child's eyes, for as adults we have lost our wonderment about the world around us.

6TH GRADE

would refrain from making negative comments to children such as, "You are ugly," "You are dumb and can't learn," "Why can't you ever do anything right?" etc.

KINDERGARTEN–6TH GRADE COUNSELOR

would think of *love* and *discipline* as two weights on a scale. Neither weight should tip the scale.

KINDERGARTEN–5TH GRADE COUNSELOR AND TEACHER

would spend *more* quality time with their children in a good, solid home environment. More family time together— teaching, learning, reading, playing, loving, and enjoying each other—is very important.

The time we have with our children is so short. They're not children long. We need to listen to them and teach them what is necessary for a good life, along with basic values. In doing this we need to be responsible role models whom they can trust and learn from as they grow up.

KINDERGARTEN

would cooperate with teachers more by not being two-sided. They say they will take care of problems that arise when contacted by phone, but many times nothing happens to the student. Parents just tell the children not to do that certain thing again.

Teachers' hands are tied in today's educational system. Children are free to do and say just about anything in the classroom. If parents would believe and trust teachers more and cooperate with the educational system by having a firmer discipline system in the home, I believe everyone would benefit.

When parents send children to their rooms for discipline, they usually have a choice of whether to play video games, watch TV, or listen to the CD player. Some punishment!

5TH GRADE

would help children set up routines at home that include homework.

3RD AND 4TH GRADES

would mark all students' belongings with their child's first and last name. I often feel like I'm running a flea market trying to place items from the land of the lost.

3RD GRADE

knew how much they can contribute to the educational process by volunteering to speak on their personal avocations, occupations, and experiences. Teachers appreciate parents as valuable resources.

KINDERGARTEN

# I WISH THAT PARENTS . . .

would hug and kiss their children good-bye each day and wish each child a good day! Also, parents need to check to see if (1) hair is combed, (2) teeth are brushed, (3) clothes are on with right-side out, (4) T-shirts are not of a vulgar nature, and (5) clothes fit the child properly.

This sounds like something parents naturally do, but I can't begin to tell you how many students arrive at school in a *very* unkempt manner. Many of our younger children are getting up, getting dressed on their own, and hurrying off to catch the bus while Mom is asleep.

2ND GRADE

knew that their children are a mirror image of themselves. If they do not like what they see, they need to take a good look at what they are saying and doing themselves.

ELEMENTARY GUIDANCE COUNSELOR

knew that children who enter kindergarten still sucking their thumbs, wetting their pants, eating with their hands, or picking their noses obviously are not ready to learn anything other than social skills.

KINDERGARTEN

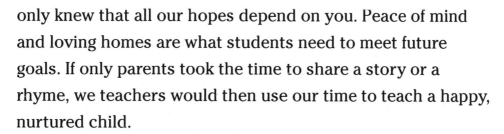

only knew that all our hopes depend on you. Peace of mind and loving homes are what students need to meet future goals. If only parents took the time to share a story or a rhyme, we teachers would then use our time to teach a happy, nurtured child.

Our struggles now are often first to show them love and inner worth. If children came for education, with love of life and satisfaction, then time in school could be used for sharing, growth, and exploration.

3RD GRADE

would be more willing to help students with their homework or at least help them come up with more original excuses for it not being done.

5TH GRADE

had to be a school board member, administrator, and teacher before becoming a parent.

KINDERGARTEN–12TH GRADE PRINCIPAL

could realize that learning to draw is an attainable skill. Of course, some are naturally better than others, but everyone can improve. I'd love it if parents would let their children know this, instead of telling them that they are hopeless at art (or anything else).

6TH–8TH GRADE ART

# I WISH THAT PARENTS . . .

would not try to relive their school years through their children.

K–12TH GRADE MUSIC

would invite their children to go for a little walk after supper instead of heading straight for the couch and the television. Even just a 15–20 minute walk would give them more energy and quality communication time. Try it, you'll like it!

HIGH SCHOOL P.E.

could substitute teach at least three days. Then they could have paper balls thrown at them, firecrackers set off at their feet, or a boy drop his pants in class. Parents would then understand the stress we face.

9TH–12TH GRADE SOCIAL STUDIES

# I WISH THAT PARENTS . . .

knew how much early adolescents need and crave quality time with their parents, but are reluctant to communicate that need to them.

7TH–8TH GRADE COUNSELOR

would realize that *listening* to children is more important than talking.

7TH–9TH GRADE ENGLISH

knew that their children's lives are a part of our lives. They are not "a job" that we can leave behind at the end of the day. Their faces, their voices, their laughter, and their tears go home with us at night. The children have changed and shaped our lives forever, as we have theirs.

4TH GRADE

would not "help" their children too much. When a parent intervenes in a child's task by taking over or doing it for him, the parent is robbing the child of self-esteem. The message is clear: "You are not capable. You are not competent."

Good parenting is like good teaching. The teacher doesn't do it for the student. The teacher guides, offers suggestions, but then stands back so that the student can reap the rewards or deal with the consequences of his own actions. Parents need to guide but not take over.

ELEMENTARY PRINCIPAL

would teach their kid(s) a lifelong rule:

Don't hurt people on the inside or the outside.

6TH–8TH GRADE SPECIAL EDUCATION

would realize that teaching is the only profession whereby its clients feel they know as much as the experts in the field.

3RD GRADE

knew the value of the creative arts for involving the whole child in the learning process, and that the arts permanently affect the memory of facts, self-esteem, problem solving, and love of learning.

ELEMENTARY ART

would concentrate on the strengths of their children, encourage their children to be thoughtful and considerate of others, and choose few and only very important battles with their children.

KINDERGARTEN–8TH GRADE COUNSELOR

# I WISH THAT PARENTS . . .

would realize how painful it can be when invitations to birthday parties are distributed at school and some of the class members do not receive an invitation.

4TH GRADE

would allow their children more time to grow up slowly and naturally. There is such beauty in the teachable spirit of a child who is trusting and spontaneous. The push to achieve, compete, and succeed often crushes the bloom of a child too early and that special time is lost, never to be found again.

3RD GRADE

would ask their children more questions about life.

4TH GRADE

knew that teachers despise giving F's. Somebody involved has definitely failed—the teacher himself, the student, or the parent. Plus, F's usually require a conference of some kind, another thing teachers despise.

7TH AND 8TH GRADE ENGLISH AND JOURNALISM

knew that on the days of parent-teacher conferences, I and other special-area teachers feel as lonely and unimportant as Maytag repairmen. It would be great if the parents of my students would come by, even if only to say hello and get acquainted.

KINDERGARTEN–6TH GRADE MUSIC

would give their children a hug before they go to school so their day starts with a touch of love (*especially* high school children).

11TH AND 12TH GRADE PHYSICS

# I WISH THAT PARENTS . . .

would realize that students with less than a C average should not be working September–June to support a 4-wheel habit. Grades and education are number *one* priority. They have the rest of their life to work for others. School is the job they work for themselves. A good education is their pay.

11TH AND 12TH GRADE GOVERNMENT AND HISTORY

would check their kids' pockets before washing the pants so that the homework assignment that was folded to fit there, instead of in a notebook, would not fall apart while I am grading it.

10TH GRADE BIOLOGY

knew that keeping classroom order while trying to be fair to every student is like trying to pop all the corn without burning any of the kernels.

HIGH SCHOOL FRENCH AND JOURNALISM

would stop ramming "ABC's and 123's" down the throats of 3-and 4-year-olds. When these children go to kindergarten, this is where they can begin to learn ABC's and 123's.

I recommend parents talk to their young children using good vocabulary, read to them, and let them play outdoors with water, mud, sand, swing sets. Give them play dough, watercolors, finger paint. Shaving cream is wonderful to play with. Let them be free in their play.

PRE-KINDERGARTEN

(and teachers) were familiar with research on personality types, brain strengths, and learning styles *and* would apply that knowledge to their children (and students). As simple a solution as providing a rocking chair for a kinesthetic learner greatly increases opportunities for success.

11TH AND 12TH GRADE ENGLISH AND JOURNALISM

# I WISH THAT PARENTS . . .

would kiss their children good-bye in the morning when the children leave for school. That way the parents might catch the "bad breath" problem so many kids have due to poor dental hygiene. Some days the odors are overpowering!

7TH AND 8TH GRADE LANGUAGE ARTS

would more closely monitor after-school employment and other extracurricular activities to protect a student's right to an education. Only when parents realize a child's "job" is school can educational standards be raised.

10TH AND 12TH GRADE ENGLISH

would realize that a seventh-grade boy who surreptitiously carves a male penis out of styrofoam in science class is a normal teenager—*not* a "sexual deviant" (his mother's words).

7TH GRADE LANGUAGE ARTS

37

# I WISH THAT PARENTS . . .

would become more involved in the daily activities of their children. Although I teach the older high school students, they are still children and they need the supervision, support, and involvement of their parents in their lives. It amazes me to hear the stories of their wild weekends, what they do when their parents are out of town or at work, how they spend their allowances, the number of hours they are allowed to socialize or date during the week (as well as the number of hours some must work), what they drank/smoked/took this morning before they came to school, and the list goes on.

It is a wonder some of these students make it to school in one piece. Don't their parents know (or care) what these children do in their spare time? For those parents who are involved, I commend you. I know that it is hard to find quality time to spend with your children when you have so many other responsibilities. But this time is an investment that will provide dividends for the rest of your lives and the lives of your children.

9TH–12TH GRADE COMPUTER SCIENCE

•————— 🎓 —————•

knew that middle-level kids are certifiably berserk! They are wonderfully challenging, and they'll be adults all too soon! I wish parents knew how much teachers really enjoy their jobs and the kids they work with and that we don't have time or energy to make life difficult or pick on one particular kid. Perspective is everything!

6TH GRADE

•————— 🎓 —————•

would realize the similarity between a spoiled child and a rotten egg. No one wants to handle either one!

10TH–12TH GRADE SOCIAL STUDIES

# I WISH THAT PARENTS . . .

knew that octopuses are seldom granted teaching certificates. Since teachers have only one set of hands, your child should be taught the "basic" skills of zipping or fastening coats and jeans/pants, as well as tying shoes, before they enroll in school. Sometimes cute overalls or jumpers are difficult for young children to manage by themselves.

1ST GRADE

would take time to write a letter of introduction regarding their child. You might tell me your child's favorite hobbies, her worst subjects, and your own desires for your child in my classroom. This would help me meet the needs of your child all that much sooner!

9TH–12TH GRADE ENGLISH

knew the following math rules:

*Add 4* to the number of days in advance of the due date that your child claims the teacher first assigned a project;

*Subtract 5* from all test scores reported by your child;

*Multiply by 3* the number of homework assignments your child thinks he missed during each grading period;

*Divide by 2* the amount of time your student claims to have spent on homework preparation;

*Factor in* always that you and the teacher are both working toward the same goal: the successful education of your child in a caring and challenging environment.

9TH–12TH GRADE FRENCH

# I WISH THAT PARENTS . . .

could appreciate the unique individuals that are in a kindergarten class. These children are always forgiving, willing to share, and eager to help one another. They are friendly and caring, accept praise and criticism gracefully, can accept others, and can work hand in hand in harmony with each other. Do we, as adults, have these qualities?

KINDERGARTEN

knew how much their children "make my day." They say things that are priceless. They are at an awkward stage in growth, so sometimes they "fall" out of their seats and we all have a great time laughing at ourselves. Mostly, I wish parents knew how privileged I feel to have their children and see in them that there *is* hope for our future.

3RD GRADE

knew that *consistency* should be the most important word in a parent's vocabulary. A parent should ask of himself, "Am I consistent in my expectations, consequences, love, and in what I say and do?"

KINDERGARTEN–5TH GRADE COUNSELOR AND TEACHER

would not come to school upset and rowdy. They should wait until they are calm and ready to settle down to discuss a problem.

2ND GRADE

would put the dog away during homework sessions so he wouldn't eat so many assignments!

5TH GRADE

would learn that their child's poor work or bad behavior is not going to be excused by saying, "He didn't act like this last year. He used to make straight A's." Don't they know that we can easily talk to the former teacher? Sometimes, their former teachers tell us that they heard the same excuse from the parents!

ELEMENTARY LEARNING DISABILITIES

knew that I do not need to know the gory details of a sickness in an absent note. They will write things like, "vomited on his pillow," or "coughing up mucous all night." A simple "stomach virus" will do the trick.

2ND GRADE

would treat each of their children as unique individuals rather than compare siblings to each other.

4TH–8TH GRADE ESL (ENGLISH AS A SECOND LANGUAGE)

# I WISH THAT PARENTS . . .

would remember that "we are what we eat." A child's behavior is definitely affected by what she consumes. Soda, candy, cookies, and the like hinder students from performing at their best.

PRE-KINDERGARTEN

could see just how bright their children's faces get when they receive a positive comment from a teacher. That look makes a teacher's day. I wonder how many parents ever see that look.

9TH–12TH GRADE SKILLS AND HEALTH

knew just a little of what their child's teachers do for them. We not only teach the child but we're their friend, counselor, companion, playmate, role model, and on and on. And we usually love every minute of it.

5TH GRADE

# I WISH THAT PARENTS . . .

would be "parents" rather than try to be their child's "friend." Their child already has enough friends. Their child needs guidance and discipline.

3RD GRADE

would not send juice boxes with straws in small children's lunches. They make fantastic squirt guns, and we wind up with rivers of juice soaking the lunch table and the children.

PRE-KINDERGARTEN

would take the time to look over their children's assignments and read with them. This keeps parents in touch with what the children are doing and how they are progressing. It also shows the children that parents consider this important.

4TH GRADE

# I WISH THAT PARENTS . . .

would be good role models for their children by turning off the television and opening up a good book!

7TH GRADE READING

would retain clearer memories of their teen years. Perhaps then they would recall the times when all they wanted and needed was someone to listen. The children haven't changed.

10TH–11TH GRADE HISTORY

would send their children to school with a desire to learn, a respect for all people, the ability to be self-disciplined, and a desire to contribute to their own learning. Parents should also be willing to accept responsibility for their child's actions and participate in making changes in unacceptable behavior.

9TH–12TH GRADE SOCIAL SCIENCE

# I WISH THAT PARENTS . . .

knew what a kind word, a touch, or a look do for their children.

11TH–12TH GRADE HOME ECONOMICS

would stay married to each other long enough to shepherd their offspring through school. What an amazing difference it makes when a loving and caring couple spend a minimum of fifteen minutes a day actively involved in their children's lives, both academic and nonacademic. The sons who throw baseballs with their moms and dads probably won't throw knives at rival gang members. The daughters who receive loving affection from mom and dad won't seek it in the form of countless brief physical relationships.

11TH–12TH GRADE ENGLISH

# I WISH THAT PARENTS . . .

could see how their "perfect kids" really behave at school. I understand that their children would "never" lie or cheat or talk back, but I think seeing their darlings (unobserved, of course) could be an eye-opener for them.

9TH GRADE ENGLISH

would take one minute of each precious day and ask their child the following question: "How was your day at school?" Response to this question allows interaction between the child and parent on the student's education and learning. In time that one minute will evolve into many minutes.

10TH–12TH GRADE HEALTH AND P.E.

would not tell their children it is OK to be bad in math because the parent was. The ability to do math is not genetic.

7TH AND 8TH GRADE MATH

# I WISH THAT PARENTS . . .

would accept their children as they are rather than put unrealistic expectations on them. Love and acceptance build a child's self-esteem, which enhances confidence.

1ST–5TH GRADES

would send their children to school ready to learn. Children need to be adequately fed and clothed before they arrive in the classroom. Students should come to school with respect for knowledge and a good attitude for learning. This *must* come from the home.

4TH GRADE

would all realize that they are teachers, too, and that we teachers must be parents at times. We are simply working different shifts.

4TH GRADE

would not send their little ones to school if they are not feeling well. Sometimes our school nurse sends a child home with a temperature of 102 degrees, and the child is right back the next day.

KINDERGARTEN

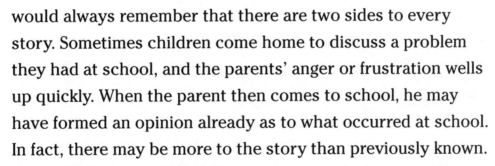

would always remember that there are two sides to every story. Sometimes children come home to discuss a problem they had at school, and the parents' anger or frustration wells up quickly. When the parent then comes to school, he may have formed an opinion already as to what occurred at school. In fact, there may be more to the story than previously known.

Parents, please remember to hear your child's story, but also the other one waiting for you at school.

5TH GRADE

would recognize the importance of reading to their children at a very early age. Six-months-old is not too soon. While reading to and with their child after she starts school is beneficial, it is too late to make up for time lost in language development. Language-deficient children struggle when learning to read.

2ND GRADE

would give us *more* "warm fuzzies." Just a positive comment once in a while would keep the fire going a long time. We do so many extra things that go unappreciated.

I like to send notes home about "good" things that happen to children. My motto is "CATCH THEM BEING GOOD!"

2ND GRADE

knew that "play" develops pathways of learning in the brain.

KINDERGARTEN

realized that peer pressure is stronger than anyone comprehends.

10TH GRADE SPEECH

---

would realize that they are a child's first and most important teacher and that their good example is the best teaching technique that their child can experience. Parents are responsible for their children.

PRE-KINDERGARTEN–5TH GRADES

---

would give their children selfless and unconditional love, model good citizenship and responsibility, and teach them values, morals, and respect for God, human life, and the environment.

Help them set priorities for their education and future so that they can be contributors to, not "takers" from, society.

11TH GRADE ENGLISH

would play—rhythmically, safely, lovingly—with their children a few minutes each day. This teaches coordination to a growing child as well as safe touch and physical parameters.

KINDERGARTEN–8TH GRADES

would be more assertive with their children. Children need, and want, limits. Too many parents let their children make decisions that children are too inexperienced to make. Sometimes, JUST SAY NO!

4TH GRADE

would impose limits on TV and video games. Try to spend more time reading together, in the same room silently or orally to one another. If it is asking too much to read together daily, then do it at least weekly.

4TH GRADE

# I WISH THAT PARENTS . . .

would realize that they, themselves, are the real heroes—the vivid role models for their adolescent children. One only has to read writing assignments I have given high school students throughout my eight years of teaching to understand how significant parents are to their teens.

9TH–11TH GRADE ENGLISH

would teach their children to ignore negative remarks, such as name calling. Teach them to talk about disagreements or offenses with the other person. Teach them to resolve conflicts peacefully.

4TH GRADE

would eat lunch at school with their child at least once a semester.

2ND GRADE

would remember that public school is not a "substitute parent." If parents do not do their part first, many students just never catch up.

3RD GRADE

would recognize that physical education is a vital and important part of their child's education. Too often, parents look at P.E. as nothing more than a supervised recess. As a physical education teacher, I spend countless hours planning and implementing ideas and techniques to foster the total development of each child. Unfortunately, these same parents only remember when they were in school and the "ole coach" just rolled out the ball during P.E.

KINDERGARTEN–5TH GRADES

# I WISH THAT PARENTS . . .

would offer reading tutorial help within their child's classroom for anyone needing it.

2ND GRADE

understood that friendship with their child means creating a true foundation of love, guidance, and discipline, not just striving to make your child "like" you.

9TH–12TH GRADE HISTORY

could be a fly on the wall and see how their children really act away from home. Parents would be amazed at the different personalities that emerge throughout the day.

11TH GRADE ENGLISH

# I WISH THAT PARENTS . . .

knew how much teachers would like to hear from them. It's a joy to receive a parent's phone call!

6TH AND 7TH GRADE WORLD CULTURES

knew that a student's learning ability can be enhanced by using as many of the senses as possible. For example, by reading an assignment orally, a child uses the senses of hearing and seeing. Creativity also increases memory retention during study.

6TH–8TH GRADE LIBRARY AND SCIENCE

would realize that even the "at-risk" students who seemingly don't care about school desperately wish their parents would take an interest in their school activities.

10TH–12TH GRADE TUTOR FOR MATH AND ENGLISH

would show RESPECT for education:

**R**ead with children

**E**ncourage them to do their best

**S**et television limitations

**P**raise children's efforts

**E**xplore their interests

**C**reate a good study environment at home

**T**ell teachers you appreciate them

1ST GRADE

would stop buying expensive toys for their child to bring to school, while whining that there is no money for paper, pencil, scissors, glue, and crayons.

2ND GRADE

59

could spend a typical day with a teacher. The day would begin in the classroom, long before the students arrive, where the parent could observe the teacher's preparations for the day. During the course of the day, they would observe the many roles performed by the teacher: educator, parent, disciplinarian, counselor, mediator, psychologist, and friend. The day would end about 9:00 P.M. in the evening in the teacher's home when the stack of student's tests and papers is graded and packed up in preparation for the next day's round of challenges.

1ST–5TH GRADES

would start parenting! It's not a popularity contest, rather an obligation to instill, encourage, and foster healthy emotional, moral, physical, and educational well-being in their children.

9TH–12TH GRADE COUNSELOR

# I WISH THAT PARENTS . . .

would remember that the most important thing a father or mother can do for their children is to show love and respect toward each other. Love needs to be modeled.

KINDERGARTEN–6TH GRADE GUIDANCE COUNSELOR

would not buy their children "novelty" school supplies that look like toys, such as extra-long pencils with loops and shapes on the end. Not only are these more expensive, they are a hindrance to learning when children are distracted from valuable learning time "playing" with their pencils instead of writing with them.

4TH GRADE

knew how many written and verbal communications they never receive from their middle and high school children.

KINDERGARTEN–8TH GRADES

would realize that there are three sides to every conflict: your side, my side, and the right side. Parents should get all the facts and then try to resolve conflicts to everyone's best interest.

2ND GRADE

were able to observe the classroom or even substitute teach for an hour or so to get the real effect of the tasks of the teachers.

4TH–5TH GRADES

would not come to school in the middle of a class and expect us to be able to drop everything to have a conference with them.

3RD GRADE

would teach their little boys to "aim to please behind closed doors." In many cases, the kindergarten bathrooms are inside the classrooms, so along with television we have "smellyvision."

KINDERGARTEN

remembered that kids need to play and to be left alone so they can think and ponder and grow. They need to be allowed to grow—not forced to grow up.

5TH GRADE

believed that teachers are not out to "get" their children or make their lives miserable. Why can't they believe that we want only what is best for their children and that we work for their children's success?

4TH GRADE

# I WISH THAT PARENTS . . .

would heed the rumor that kids learn better with a sense of humor.

6TH–8TH GRADES

spent more time talking with young adolescents about their concerns and worries. Relationships, growth, body image, and acceptance are major concerns of middle school students. Parents can reassure their children by talking with them and communicating their love and understanding.

8TH GRADE LANGUAGE ARTS

would remember that school does not become important to the child until she knows it is important to her parents.

3RD–5TH GRADES

would remember that it is in our errors that we do the most learning. What we learn from our mistakes makes the difference.

3RD GRADE

would remember to have children brush their teeth every morning *before* coming to school. It's hard to give individualized assistance to a little angel who has devil's breath.

1ST GRADE

would remember what their world was like when they were seven years old. That was a time when getting a math problem wrong was as devastating as the eruption of a volcano, or when accidentally wetting your pants in class made you want to crawl into the cracks of the woodwork and never come out.

1ST GRADE

understood the diversity of the children we teach today. I have taught since 1977 and have seen a tremendous growth of students coming from Mexico. Also, today's students seem to have more identifiable emotional problems. I have a responsibility to serve each child to the best of my ability, and with all these challenges come great rewards.

3RD GRADE

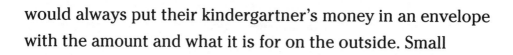

would always put their kindergartner's money in an envelope with the amount and what it is for on the outside. Small children regularly forget what the money is to be used for.

KINDERGARTEN

would relax with their children, get down on their level, and enjoy the many wonders of the world together.

KINDERGARTEN

would tell children how well they did when they finish a task—even if it's not exactly the way you wanted it done. My two-year-old was trying to help me with the dishes once and put every single dish back into the cupboard. She was so proud of herself that I made no mention that the dishes were still dirty.

1ST AND 2ND GRADES

would remember that in the presence of "little ears," a positive attitude and respect toward educators would be a sure "sound" hit.

1ST GRADE

would remember that learning is a shared responsibility. Children do not learn everything in school, but what they do learn there needs reinforcing and rewarding at home.

1ST GRADE

knew how a few kind words from them can go a long way to make teachers feel appreciated.

2ND GRADE

of middle school students would give us credit for TRYING to keep up with their child's hormone growth spurts. They're speeding and we're in the slow traffic lane.

JUNIOR HIGH COUNSELOR

could switch jobs with teachers for just one day and experience the realities of the classroom. I'm willing to bet that experience would generate a lot more parent participation within all schools and regenerate respect for the teaching profession.

4TH GRADE

would be more willing to help their children pursue scholarship opportunities. Unfortunately, the kids need prodding, cajoling, and encouraging to complete the tedious task of writing essays and mailing them before deadlines.

12TH GRADE ENGLISH

•———— 🎓 ————•

would remember that children are NOT little adults. Please let them experience the joy, love, and security that children so desperately need, want, and deserve! (Wouldn't you love to be a child again?)

1ST GRADE

•———— 🎓 ————•

knew that by the age of fifteen their kids have developed their full emotional capabilities; they just need experiences to temper their responses.

6TH–8TH GRADE SPECIAL EDUCATION

knew all of the good things about their kids. As adults we say that kids are very cruel. It is their own insecurities that make them that way.

6TH–8TH GRADE SPECIAL EDUCATION

knew how obnoxious children are at school when they are not disciplined at home.

5TH GRADE

understood that teachers don't like to send home negative notes. The teacher is not angry but in fact loves the child enough to take the time to inform her parents.

3RD GRADE

would admit it, correct it, forget it!

4TH GRADE

# I WISH THAT PARENTS . . .

would be informed and know what is being taught in the classes. Investigate your children's work in and out of class. Be a reading advocate and share what your children are reading. Network with the teachers and learn about your children's work habits and learning styles.

Help your children be good thinkers and problem solvers and teach them to take responsibility for their actions. Children need role models, love, patience, and a place to belong. They need someone who is there for them in all situations.

Since most parents and teachers want children to succeed, forming a partnership is the natural thing to do.

5TH GRADE

would remember that young people are like fresh cement— anything dropped on them will make a big impression.

12TH GRADE SOCIAL STUDIES

# I WISH THAT PARENTS . . .

would not write the child's book reports for them. The parents don't seem to realize that teachers can tell the difference between their work and their child's work.

*3RD GRADE*

·——— 🎓 ———·

knew that their children can learn to read as naturally as they learned to speak. In all my years of teaching (twenty-seven of them) I have never had a parent tell me, "I remember when I taught my child to talk." No, the children I have taught learned to speak by imitation and response to adults speaking to them.

If you would read to your child daily from the day they are born and show them progressively what words look like in books that you are enjoying together, their reading would come naturally. Their beginning school days would be more enjoyable and successful.

*1ST–3RD GRADE REMEDIAL READING*

# I WISH THAT PARENTS . . .

would remember that *everything* they say and do in front of their children comes to school with their children daily and reflects in their work, speech, actions, and attitude.

1ST GRADE

knew that what happens over the weekend or in the morning at home determines how the child will behave in the classroom, be it negative or positive.

9TH–12TH GRADE HOME ECONOMICS

would encourage their children to listen to all forms of music and listen with them. I wish parents would realize more is being taught in music class than just singing songs.

ELEMENTARY VOCAL MUSIC

knew that we also want the best for their children. Teachers are not the enemy. No war should be taking place. Yet, teachers must work right from the start to get some parents on our side. When the homefront and the schoolfront become allied, beautiful things take place. Why weren't parents ever mentioned in our education classes?

5TH GRADE

·——— 🎓 ———·

would consider teachers as extended family (I've been called "Mom" and "Grandma" often enough). We're with their children for at least six hours each day. If something occurs that will probably affect a child's performance (academic, social, emotional), it needs to be shared with the child's teacher.

Specifics aren't necessary. It would just be nice to know that something is going on at home before problems occur in the classroom.

4TH GRADE

knew that today (when I still have not received an educational assistant because my student enrollment does not yet warrant one) Kristin spilled green paint on the new carpet in my room while I was in the floor tracing Jessica's silhouette on butcher paper for her student-of-the-week poster. Within ten minutes Stefan had thrown up all over his cut-and-paste sheet.

Today I was patted on the behind six times hard because a child wanted my attention. I administered three bandages, called two mothers during my break, and refereed an argument over whose yellow crayon was still on the floor when it was time to go.

Tomorrow I will arise at 5:30, leave my home at 7:20, and start the process all over again. And why? The answer is easy—because these children, my "babies," fulfill far more in my life than I can ever fulfill in theirs.

KINDERGARTEN

remembered that C is average. Their child has learned the material as well as the average (typical) child learns it. Remember, a C child is also creative and capable.

2ND–5TH GRADE RESOURCE

would remember that they are the parents, not the children. Children need to be children and must learn to accept and live by rules. Parents must accept this responsibility and be firm, loving, understanding, and fair.

3RD–6TH GRADES CHAPTER 1

knew how much uncompensated time teachers spend in preparation for instruction. It is important to *me* that *I* do an excellent job.

2ND GRADE

# I WISH THAT PARENTS . . .

would realize that although we love and do our best for their children, we cannot be, and should not be expected to be, a surrogate or foster parent to our students while they are in our classes.

It is very difficult to do any good parenting or undo any bad parenting in our classrooms in addition to teaching. Parents need to be parents at home so teachers can be teachers at school.

6TH–8TH GRADE TUTORING PROGRAM

realized that giving and hugging are the easy parts of loving. Disciplining and following through on consequences are the difficult but equally important part of loving.

6TH GRADE

would make a point to find some time in your schedule for your children. They need you, your support, and your concern, whether or not they outwardly show their appreciation. Become aware of their school activities and responsibilities and encourage their involvement in meaningful activities after school. These activities could include scouting, church groups, a small part-time job (to teach responsibility), or volunteer work.

Be an example for your children, for they may someday raise a family of their own and will look to their family experiences for guidance. Remember, your time is an investment in the current and future successes of your children.

9TH–12TH GRADE COMPUTER SCIENCE

would listen to their kids!

3RD AND 4TH GRADES

would return to the "old fashioned idea" that if you got into trouble at school—you would be in twice as much trouble at home. The current thinking appears to be, "Let's go to school and see why they're picking on my child."

4TH GRADE

could know how truly important a part they play in their child's developing a lifetime of asking questions, which begins with "The Great Inquisition of Childhood." Why is the sky blue? Is it morning in Australia? Where *is* Australia? How are mountains made? Why do people revolt?

   Parents must encourage and engage the natural questioning of children. Then parents need to know that when they are weary and out of answers, they must remember to say, "Go and ask your teacher that question."

1ST GRADE

# I WISH THAT PARENTS . . .

realized the wonderful opportunity they have to teach their children about the world in which they live. Take advantage of nature, books, etc. Leave the skill and drill of letters and numbers until later. Your child will benefit greatly from the natural learning experiences you provide.

1ST GRADE

would realize that not all students are going to college, and that many people make an excellent living working with their hands. Vocational subjects require academic skills and should not be a dumping ground for those who can't succeed in other areas. If a student hasn't mastered those basic academic skills, then he will in all likelihood have problems in the vocational area as well.

9TH–12TH GRADE AUTOMOTIVE TECHNOLOGY

would allow teachers to use their individual talents. Many parents think that if a teacher does not teach the same way that some other teacher does, then she (or he) is not doing an efficient job. Children need exposure to various learning techniques, and often parents thwart a teacher's talent to do so.

1ST GRADE

knew that if they really listened with their hearts to their children, they would learn a lot about what's really important in life. I'm talking about focused, active listening that enables the parent to become a part of the child's world. This should occur daily. It would save thousands of dollars in therapy bills later in life.

3RD GRADE

would give their children family customs and traditions to pass from generation to generation—the silly songs to sing on long auto trips, the special cookies served only on holidays, the unique secrets of the family tree—these will preserve the qualities which define who they are.

KINDERGARTEN

realized each child is an entire unique creature—no two are alike. They do not act alike so they should not be treated alike or expected to act alike.

KINDERGARTEN–12TH GRADE COUNSELOR

knew that children live up to the expectations you set for them. How are your expectations for your child—too high, too low, or no expectations at all?

3RD GRADE

could be "teacher for a day." I think they would have a better appreciation for schools and teachers if they spent some time in the classroom dealing with the daily mishaps and challenges.

KINDERGARTEN

would think when communicating negative comments to teachers by either phone or note. Please do not let your child see or hear you raise your voice to the teacher. This gives the student the impression that it's okay to yell at the teacher.

What we really like to see is the teacher and parent working together in a partnership for the good of all. How would the parent feel if she were being yelled at at work in front of her own peers or children? *Nothing* positive ever comes from this kind of communication.

3RD GRADE

# I WISH THAT PARENTS . . .

would respect and treat their child's teacher with the same professional courtesy they avail to their dentist, minister, or pediatrician.

ELEMENTARY PRINCIPAL

would only believe half of what they hear about school; and I would, likewise, believe only half of what I hear about home. Teachers and parents need to stay in close touch with each other to know what is really going on because a child's point of view is not always accurate.

5TH GRADE

realized that there are lowercase letters in the alphabet. Many children come to kindergarten spelling their name in all capitals, and they have to relearn their name all over again!

KINDERGARTEN

# I WISH THAT PARENTS . . .

would take responsibility for their part in their child's education. If families don't value reading and education at home, their children won't value it in school. If children aren't disciplined and respectful at home, they will be discipline problems in school.

6TH–8TH GRADE LITERACY AND SOCIAL STUDIES

knew of all the great, spontaneous, and brilliant ideas their child comes up with in everyday class discussions!

7TH GRADE SOCIAL STUDIES

knew how funny their children look when they first bite into a something sour, like a lemon, for their lesson about the sense of taste.

KINDERGARTEN

# I WISH THAT PARENTS . . .

would respect decisions made by teachers and realize they are made in the best interest of the child. A decision will never please all but must be respected by parents. Discipline begins at home. With the proper backing from these children's parents, we could omit most of our problems at school.

KINDERGARTEN–8TH GRADES

would become more involved with, and interact more with, the school and teachers. It seems they feel that older elementary students don't need them as much as the younger ones, but the older ones do.

4TH GRADE

would recognize that a pat on their child's back is more effective than a "pat" on the bottom.

4TH GRADE

would understand homework is not always written. Written homework is only Step 1 and the easy part. Step 2 is to study and understand the material so they know it without the crutch (that written sheet).

11TH AND 12TH GRADE SOCIAL STUDIES

were willing to allow their children to have what we in the field call "dignity of risk," an opportunity to fail *or* succeed. They have sheltered their children for so long that their progress is often hindered.

10TH–12TH GRADE SPECIAL EDUCATION

would come to events and activities that their children are involved in at the high school level.

9TH–12TH GRADE SOCIAL STUDIES

# I WISH THAT PARENTS . . .

knew we care greatly about their child. We are their biggest supporter. Teachers use much of their own money to buy positive reinforcers and projects for their classes. We spend much unpaid outside time gathering and buying materials to make our class more interesting.

4TH GRADE

knew that their children really do look up to them and want them to be the best role models. Parents need to stay attuned to their children's expectations of them and strive to be their leader, their friend, and their superstar.

8TH GRADE ENGLISH

knew that our most successful students consistently come from supportive families.

HIGH SCHOOL

# I WISH THAT PARENTS . . .

could attend school the first two weeks of every school year to familiarize themselves with subject matter, teacher expectations, and student responsibilities. This would eliminate many problems throughout the year which usually stem from some parents who feel inadequate in helping their children with homework, and/or who do not understand school policies, particularly in the area of discipline.

I realize this is an unrealistic wish, but I have adapted it by inviting parents to join my classes during a particular writing project and to learn how to write effectively along with their children. I wish more parents would accept the invitation, although I'm pleased that a few do. My biggest wish, therefore, is for more parental knowledge of and involvement in the educational lives of their children.

8TH GRADE ENGLISH

# I WISH THAT PARENTS . . .

would feel the need to be responsible for their children's education. Then they would be involved not only in overseeing their children's work and attitudes but also in actively supporting the needs of the school system.

We need to see parents as enthusiastic about an education as they are about successful sports programs.

8TH GRADE ENGLISH

would send their children off to school with a positive feeling. Let your child know that she is very special in her own unique way. Sing a special song, send a note to read later, or put a surprise in her lunchbox. Self-esteem is important for quality learning to take place.

1ST GRADE

# I WISH THAT PARENTS . . .

would remember that *they* are their child's first, most influential, and most important teacher. The examples they set for their children make a lifelong impact upon them.

6TH GRADE SCIENCE

· —— 🎓 —— ·

knew that making excuses for your child only teaches them how to make excuses for failure later in life!

3RD GRADE

· —— 🎓 —— ·

knew how special their kids are. Some don't even have a clue.

12TH GRADE ENGLISH

· —— 🎓 —— ·

would let their children do their own reports, visual aids, etc. Kids should have fun, too!

4TH GRADE

# I WISH THAT PARENTS . . .

would teach their children this important Rule for Happiness:

> Those who give a maximum effort will be the real bene-
> ficiaries of life and will receive the self-satisfaction that
> allows them to live happily with themselves and others.

I have observed through the years that some students are happier than others. I have also observed that some students work harder than others to pass. Some "get by" while others give a maximum effort, yet all students will share some of the same rewards of life.

We often confuse *life* with *living* and *getting by* with really *achieving*. There is a difference. We find more satisfaction and joy from what we give than from what we get. When students learn this important truth, a happy, rewarding life will follow.

9TH–12TH GRADE BIOLOGY

# I WISH THAT PARENTS . . .

would remember that a child is a human being who makes mistakes (just like parents), is still learning to be human (just like parents), needs lot of love and support (just like parents), knows how to play better than parents, and should not be compared to anyone else.

10TH–12TH GRADE HOME ECONOMICS

would realize that *they* are their children's first and most impressionable teachers. Schoolteachers get children as students after their formative years, after their personalities have been developed, and usually after four or five years of being taught, trained, and inculcated by parents or other caretakers. Children bring to school with them what they have been taught at home.

7TH AND 8TH GRADE LANGUAGE ARTS

# I WISH THAT PARENTS . . .

knew that everybody who has sat in a classroom doesn't know how to teach. Most people don't realize what teaching is like from my side of the desk. Recently, while sitting in a writing lab with about $100,000 worth of equipment, a lady told me that all a real teacher needs is a piece of chalk.

12TH GRADE ENGLISH

would teach their offspring lifelong custodial skills such as placing trash in the garbage cans as opposed to dropping it shy by six inches or so. I'd love to have students trained in keeping their work spaces clean rather than leaving messages on the desks for anyone who sits there.

9TH–12TH GRADE ART/PUBLICATIONS

would realize that teachers do not have horns, fangs, or claws. (Well, *most* teachers don't!) We're just average people trying to do what is best for their child. So, they should come visit us and our class at least two or three times a semester. It all works best when we all work together!

6TH GRADE

would use correct grammar. Is "There is three pencils" going to become standard English in the next century?

7TH AND 8TH GRADE LANGUAGE ARTS

would demand respect for authority and property. My students tell me that their parents allow them to sit on dinner tables, put their dirty feet in chairs, and say, "yeah," "huh," "nope," "naw," and "yo" to them.

MIDDLE SCHOOL HOME ECONOMICS

# I WISH THAT PARENTS . . .

would help develop an inquiry and discovery attitude in children during the preschool and early school years. Girls need to know how capable they can become in the sciences.

10TH GRADE BIOLOGY

would build their child's self-concept. Kids should feel like a balloon in the Macy's parade.

4TH GRADE

would realize that teachers cannot remember what Johnny did or exactly what was said on the third Monday of last month.

KINDERGARTEN–3RD GRADE SPECIAL EDUCATION

would let their children act their age and not say, "I wish you'd grow up!"

2ND GRADE

# I WISH THAT PARENTS . . .

knew how appreciated and valued they are to teachers when they send us a well-behaved student possessing a positive attitude. These students are priceless gifts for their fortunate teachers. Day after day, these precious gems follow directions, complete their tasks, and unobtrusively exhibit their self-control.

Many times these special students are neglected when the teacher's attention is diverted. This distresses the teacher because the very ones who deserve the best are deprived by the few who do not reach the benchmark. If you happen to be a parent who has sent us one of these prized children, thank you! After all, children are a reflection of their home life.

5TH GRADE

would be required to substitute teach for at least one week. Complaints about teachers would decrease rapidly!

KINDERGARTEN–5TH GRADE CURRICULUM COORDINATOR

97

realized how dramatically kids have changed since they were in school. In order to understand the kinds of challenges today's teachers face, all parents should visit classrooms often and "walk in our shoes."

7TH GRADE READING/ENGLISH

would remember the contribution of special subject teachers toward a child's overall success in school. Librarians and art, music, computer, health, and physical education teachers all deserve thanks when a child succeeds.

3RD AND 4TH GRADE MEDIA SPECIALIST

knew how each word they say to their child affects him and how arguments between people at home affect a child's life at school.

3RD GRADE

would stay involved in their children's education and would keep the lines of communication open with their children. These were the two most pressing concerns among students polled in our junior and senior high school.

HIGH SCHOOL BUSINESS EDUCATION/JOURNALISM

knew how much students need praise. An abundance of praise can motivate them to do nearly anything. Students are like new plants . . . without praise (sunshine), they cannot thrive and grow.

10TH AND 12TH GRADE ENGLISH

would remember that most teachers enter the classroom each day with determination, enthusiasm, and love.

3RD GRADE

# I WISH THAT PARENTS . . .

realized "smart" is something that is learned. While parents and teachers are a team, it's the parent that sets the tone for the child's success: by being concerned, by being interested, and by making the child responsible for her learning and behavior.

KINDERGARTEN–6TH GRADE ART

would allow their children to accept responsibility for their own actions and inactions.

5TH–6TH GRADES

would stay responsible for their children even after they drop them at the school doors. I wish that parents would become part of their children's education. Get involved! Be there!

8TH GRADE MATH

# I WISH THAT PARENTS . . .

realized that when they tell their child long enough that he is stupid, he will believe it. If, however, they offer encouragement and guidance when needed, the child will have the confidence to try and succeed because he will believe in himself.

5TH GRADE

would remember how it was when they were young! Children these days have many pressures put on them by peers that lead to big trouble. If parents would not just try to be parents but also good listeners, I think a lot of the trouble would end.

The child is the automobile and the parents have to be its steering wheel!

7TH AND 8TH GRADES

would tell their child a riddle or joke before leaving in the mornings so the child would have a smile on his face when he gets to school.

3RD GRADE

would teach their children better health habits, such as how to blow and wipe their nose, wash their hands, clean food from their face after lunch, and throw away used tissues.

3RD GRADE

would treat their marriage with the same sense of thoughtfulness and practicality they do the acquisition of the family car. They need to discard the idea of the lease, wherein it is all too easy to walk away when any trouble happens and start all over with a new one.

ELEMENTARY ADMINISTRATION

would remember that your children are only young once. Enjoy them while you can because they will grow up much too fast. Give them your most precious gift—yourself and your love.

4TH GRADE

would "celebrate" their child's successes, regardless of size or apparent worth. What may seem unimportant to you as a parent may have significant value to your child.

KINDERGARTEN–4TH GRADE SPECIAL EDUCATION

understood that a child is a lifetime commitment. The school can never take the place of a parent and should not be expected to.

1ST–3RD GRADE CHAPTER 1 READING

# I WISH THAT PARENTS . . .

knew how much teachers *care* and how much time they spend trying to meet the needs of their students.

2ND GRADE

would teach their children how to blow their noses and tie their shoes before they start to school. This would save many time-consuming moments with my preschoolers.

KINDERGARTEN

would take an interest in their child's work once they start to school and let them know they are wonderful in so many ways! Too often, students fail to hear something positive about themselves. We focus on what they can't do or aren't doing instead of what they do know.

KINDERGARTEN

# I WISH THAT PARENTS . . .

knew how important they are to their children and would take a more active role in their parenting responsibilities. I feel that too many children have too much free time and too little guidance at home.

9TH–12TH GRADE HEALTH

would plan a weekly walk with their children. What they may learn about their child in one mile could be more valuable than all the health benefits combined.

1ST–3RD GRADE P.E.

knew that teaching isn't as easy as it looks. Teachers are required to know more now than ever before and are expected to teach many areas other than just those they are licensed to teach.

11TH AND 12TH GRADE SOCIAL STUDIES

knew that the child they have at home may take on a whole new personality at school.

7TH GRADE

knew that their children need to accept more responsibility for their work and should be held accountable for their behavior.

2ND GRADE

knew that I am much more than a teacher. I am a counselor, housekeeper, nurse, encyclopedia, travel agent, as well as a teacher for subjects other than my own. It challenges me every day and I love it.

6TH–12TH GRADE VOCAL MUSIC

## AFTERWORD

*When we conceived this book, we wanted to avoid a heavy "theory of education" or serious message book. We asked teachers for brief responses and encouraged them to look for creative, humorous messages. But this teacher's experience is so compelling and relevant, we felt it must be included.*

**I WISH THAT PARENTS** would strongly evaluate the role sports play in their son or daughter's life. As a student athlete and as a teacher I feel compelled to share just a few of my personal experiences and observations. If I reach just one parent, it will all be worthwhile.

As a student athlete, I was subjected to pressure of

indescribable proportions. Our lives revolved around and were dominated by sports—in particular, football. The message sent to athletes openly and covertly was that sports—this week's game, the season—are more important than education.

My colleagues and I were permitted and encouraged to take watered-down courses of study. Intro I. Intro II. Never did I study nor make any effort to cheat, and yet I almost always attained good grades.

I learned it was OK to partake in illegal practice sessions and OK to play in Friday's game even though I had been diagnosed earlier that week with a concussion. In general, football, not education, was important. I later received a football scholarship to a local state school and promptly quit football but remained in school. I made the dean's list that year, but nobody asked me about my educational accomplishments. What they did ask me was, why had I quit football?

I am answering them now. I quit football because I hated it. I learned to hate it even more as I struggled through my first year of college devoid of study skills and deficient of a general knowledge base. I recall a coach's son with tears streaming down his face prior to the "big" game. He told me he was afraid, that he didn't want to go out there. I remember seeing my friend in the hospital with holes drilled through his skull, having been fortunate enough to survive a broken neck. I remember my parents taxiing me here and there for sports, but just a few times do I remember impatient efforts at homework assistance.

I don't hate my parents for this. My only wish is that society in general and mothers and fathers across the world would realize what they are doing to their children. I ask you to think about how much time you spend with your child on school-related activities and compare that to your involvement in their sports activities. I ask you to evaluate why your son or daughter is playing a particular sport. Is it for the child or for you? Can he or she quit without retribution? Would your child quit if permitted?

Sports does have a role in America. It should be an active one, promoting healthy lifestyles through exercise and win-win competition. Undoubtedly, "sports" provides important opportunities for building character and improving self-concept through accomplishment. Athletics, however, is just one facet of the total person. The arts and academia are equally important to human development. My wish is for this balance.

SPECIAL EDUCATION

Judy and Tony Privett live in Slaton, Texas,
with their two children.

Dear Reader:

If you have any ideas or
experiences in education to
be considered for a future
book, please send them to:

Judy and Tony Privett
1408 Peoria
Slaton, TX 79364